DUDLEY SCHOOLS
LIBRARY SERVICE

KU-337-435

Schools Library and Information Services

S00000704383

PICTUREPEDIA

NOTE TO PARENTS

This book is part of PICTUREPEDIA, a completely
new kind of information series for children.
Its unique combination of pictures and words
encourages children to use their eyes to discover and
explore the world, while introducing them to a wealth
of basic knowledge. Clear, straightforward text
explains each picture thoroughly and provides
additional information about the topic.

'Looking it up' becomes an easy task with
PICTUREPEDIA, an ideal first reference for all types of
schoolwork. Because PICTUREPEDIA is also entertaining,
children will enjoy reading its words and looking
at its pictures over and over again. You can encourage
and stimulate further inquiry by helping your child
pose simple questions for the whole family to
'look up' and answer together.

MACHINES

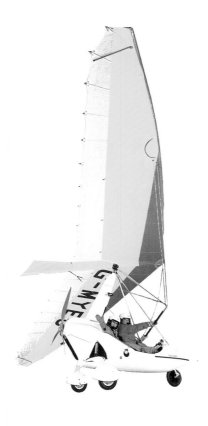

DK

DORLING KINDERSLEY

LONDON, NEW YORK, AUCKLAND
DELHI, MUNICH, SYDNEY

DK www.dk.com

First published in Great Britain in 1993
by Dorling Kindersley Limited, London

This updated edition published in 2000 by:

Dorling Kindersley Limited
9 Henrietta Street, London WC2E 8PS, Great Britain

Dorling Kindersley Publishing Pty Limited
(A.C.N. 078 414 445)
118-120 Pacific Highway, St Leonards NSW 2065, Australia

Dorling Kindersley (India) Pvt. Ltd.
102/3 Kaushalya Park, Hauz Khas, New Delhi 110016, India

Copyright © 1993 Dorling Kindersley Limited, London

All rights reserved. No part of this publication may be reproduced,
stored in a retrieval system, or transmitted in any form or by any means,
electronic, mechanical, photocopying, recording or otherwise,
without the prior written permission of the copyright owner.

A CIP catalogue record for this
book is available from the British Library.

ISBN 0 7513 6912 8

Reproduction by Colourscan, Singapore
Printed and bound by L. Rex Printing Company Limited, China

DUDLEY PUBLIC LIBRARY

704383   SCH

J621·8

MACHINES

DK

A DORLING KINDERSLEY BOOK

CONTENTS

THE FIRST
MACHINES 6

MACHINES FOR
POWER 16

MOVING ON
LAND 8

DIGGING AND
LIFTING 18

TELLING THE
TIME 20

ENGINES AND
MOTORS 10

TAKING PICTURES 22

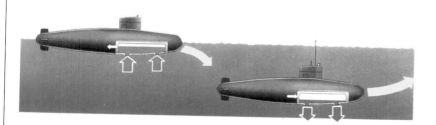

MOVING AT SEA 12

MAKING
MOVIES 24

FLYING MACHINES 14

SPREADING
THE NEWS 26

WAR MACHINES 28

HOME HELPS 38

SPYING AND SNOOPING 30

SPORTS MACHINES 40

COMPUTER MAGIC 32

ELECTRONIC GAMES 42

ROBOTS 34

MAKING MUSIC 44

FAIRGROUNDS 46

MACHINES FOR HEALTH 36

GLOSSARY & INDEX 48

THE FIRST MACHINES

People have always looked for ways of making it easier to do a task. Machines make it possible to do a task using less effort. Over 20,000 years ago, hunters invented the bow and arrow. Armed with this machine they could send a pointed stick through the air. Other machines followed. The plough was invented about 9,000 years ago, then the wheel. From scissors to screwdriver, machines are all around us now, making our lives easier.

Roll On

Wheels for transport were invented over 5,000 years ago and were very heavy. Now they are lighter. There are also wheels suitable for high-speed driving.

Bow and Arrow

The first bows were strips of wood bent into a curve with a string. When the archer pulled back the string, the wood bent so much that it sprang back as soon as he let go, shooting the arrow forwards.

The earliest wheeled vehicles had wheels made either of solid wood or of planks, so they were very heavy. They appeared in Mesopotamia over 5,000 years ago.

The Plough

Early people used to turn over the soil for planting with just a digging stick and hoe. But they eventually realized that they could turn the soil much more easily by drawing a cutting blade called a plough through it.

The Potter's Wheel

Wheels are used in many machines, not just for transport. In fact, the first wheels were probably used 5,000 years ago by potters for turning clay to make pots, and later by millers to grind corn.

The wheels used on ancient Egyptian chariots were much lighter because large sections of wood were cut away.

For thousands of years, most wheels were like this cartwheel. Its wooden spokes were surrounded by a hoop of wood, strengthened by a metal rim.

Helpful Levers

A lever is a machine that gives out more effort than you put in. When you use a pair of scissors, your effort on the handle turns the blades round the hinge, or fulcrum. This magnifies your effort giving the blades enough power to cut.

A spanner is a lever for turning a bolt very forcefully. The bolt is the fulcrum.

The top of a tap is a lever that screws up and down to control the flow of water.

The handle of a screwdriver is a lever to help you turn a screw with extra force.

Now all cars have light metal wheels with pneumatic, or air-filled, tyres. These give a much softer ride.

e very light, wire-spoked wheels w used on bicycles were first d in the early 1870s.

Racing cars have wide tyres, made of a sticky sort of rubber, to give good grip at high speeds.

MOVING ON LAND

A 19th-century horse-drawn carriage

Trevithick's carriage

Once, the only way to travel far on land was on horseback or in a horse-drawn carriage. But in 1803, Englishman Richard Trevithick built a carriage that ran on rails and was driven along by a steam engine. Motor cars first appeared in the 1860s, when petrol engines were invented. Now there are enough cars in the world to form a traffic jam stretching to the Moon and back!

Turning the Wheels

The axle turns a car's wheels. When a car turns left, the wheels on the right must travel farther than the wheels on the left, so they must turn faster. The engine is connected to the axle by a set of gears called the differential. This lets the wheels turn at slightly different speeds round corners.

Drive from the engine

Differential

Axle

As in many cars made to be driven off the road, the engine powers all four wheels.

Underneath the bonnet is a very powerful engine.

These bars protect the passengers if the car crashes and rolls over. Safety belts keep the passengers in.

The chunky tyres covered with big knobbles are ideal f[or] a good grip in mud and sand.

From Steam to Electric

Rocket, 1829

American steam locomotive, 1875

Slippery Cars

Car designers test their designs in wind tunnels to make sure the air flows smoothly over them. A good design uses less petrol. Wind tunnels have a big fan to create a strong wind. Ribbons stuck to the car show how the wind flows over it.

The Model T Ford was the first car to sell over a million.

Fun Car

Not many cars are as much fun as this beach buggy. But most cars work in much the same way, with an engine at the front to drive the wheels round.

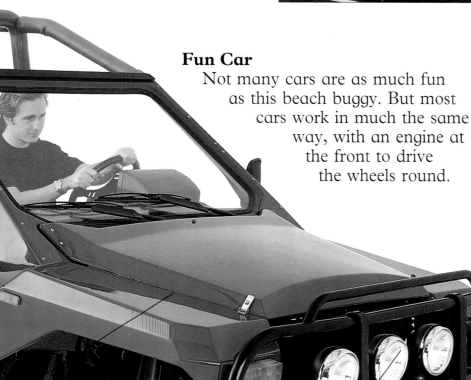

The Volkswagen Beetle was the most popular car ever made. Over 40 million were built.

The *City of Truro* was the first steam engine to reach 100 miles an hour (160 km/h).

These headlights help the driver to see at night. They must be aimed down to prevent them dazzling oncoming drivers.

The TGV is the fastest passenger train in the world. It can travel at over 300 km/h.

Mallard, 1938

Diesel-electric locomotive, 1956

ENGINES AND MOTORS

Engines and motors provide power to make things move. Motors usually run on electricity and drive small things, like hair dryers. Engines are usually more powerful and run on heat. In steam engines – the first real engines – heat boils water to make steam and the steam pushes the engine round, just as steam in a pan of boiling water pushes up the lid. Cars have 'internal combustion' engines. In these, the engine is pushed round by the gas produced from burning petrol inside the engine.

Boiler to make steam

Letting off Steam
Until about 40 years ago, brightly coloured steam traction engines like this one were often seen at fairgrounds. The traction engine drove the rides and made electricity for the lights.

Electric Power
Electric motors work by magnetism. An electric current passing through a coil of wire turns the coil into a very powerful magnet. If the coil is set between another magnet, it is driven round at great speed to power your hair dryer.

Magnet

Coil of wire spins round

Jet Power
Most modern aeroplanes have jet engines. These push a blast of hot a and other gases out at the back which drives the plane forwards at enormous speed.

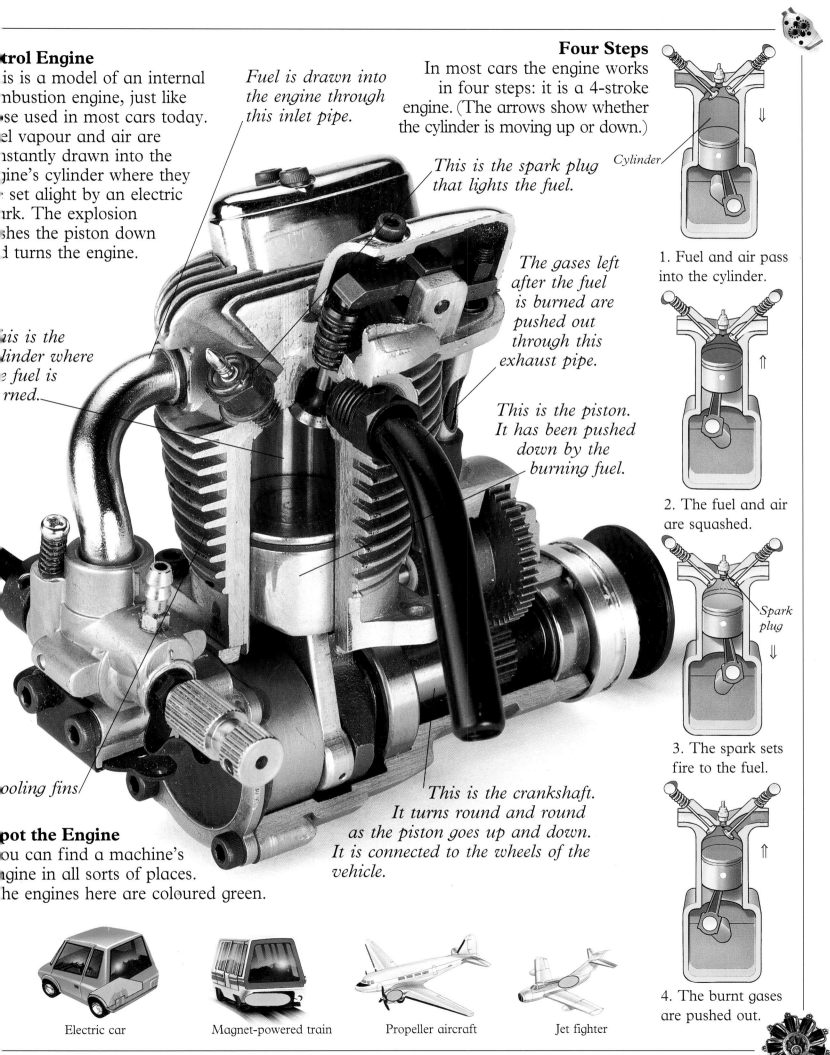

trol Engine

is is a model of an internal
nbustion engine, just like
se used in most cars today.
el vapour and air are
stantly drawn into the
gine's cylinder where they
set alight by an electric
rk. The explosion
shes the piston down
d turns the engine.

is is the
linder where
e fuel is
rned.

ooling fins

pot the Engine

ou can find a machine's
gine in all sorts of places.
he engines here are coloured green.

*Fuel is drawn into
the engine through
this inlet pipe.*

*This is the spark plug
that lights the fuel.*

*The gases left
after the fuel
is burned are
pushed out
through this
exhaust pipe.*

*This is the piston.
It has been pushed
down by the
burning fuel.*

*This is the crankshaft.
It turns round and round
as the piston goes up and down.
It is connected to the wheels of the
vehicle.*

Four Steps

In most cars the engine works
in four steps: it is a 4-stroke
engine. (The arrows show whether
the cylinder is moving up or down.)

Cylinder

1. Fuel and air pass
into the cylinder.

2. The fuel and air
are squashed.

Spark
plug

3. The spark sets
fire to the fuel.

4. The burnt gases
are pushed out.

Electric car

Magnet-powered train

Propeller aircraft

Jet fighter

11

MOVING AT SEA

Sailing Ships
For thousands of years ships only had the wind to drive them along. Big ships had tall masts with enormous sails. Now many people use sailing boats for fun.

Early ships with only the wind to drive them along were rather slow. And even the biggest of them looks small to us today. But modern ships have powerful engines and some, like supertankers, are so long that the crew needs motor scooters to get from one end to the other. Water covers three-quarters of the Earth's surface, so it is not surprising to find so many different boats and ships all over the world.

Why Don't Ships Sink?

Even though they are heavy, ships float because their hulls are hollow and full of air. A ball of plasticine sinks, but if you hollow it into a bowl shape, it will float just like a boat.

Ball of plasticine sinks

Bowl of plasticine floats

SeaCat is steered by a pair of waterjets on each side.

There are two engines in each of the side hulls.

Going Down!

A submarine dives by pushing air out of and taking water into special tanks. The water makes the submarine so heavy it sinks.

Coming Up!

It comes up again by taking compressed air into the tanks to force the water out. The submarine gets lighter and floats up.

Cars are stowed on one of the lower decks.

Big Cats

Catamarans have two hulls to help them go faster than ordinary boats. The SeaCat is the largest high-speed catamaran ever built. can take 450 people a 80 cars across the English Channel in jus under an hour.

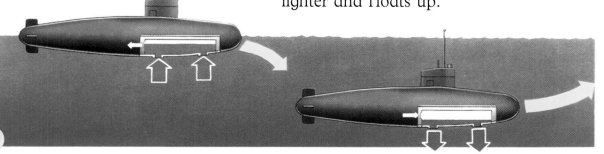

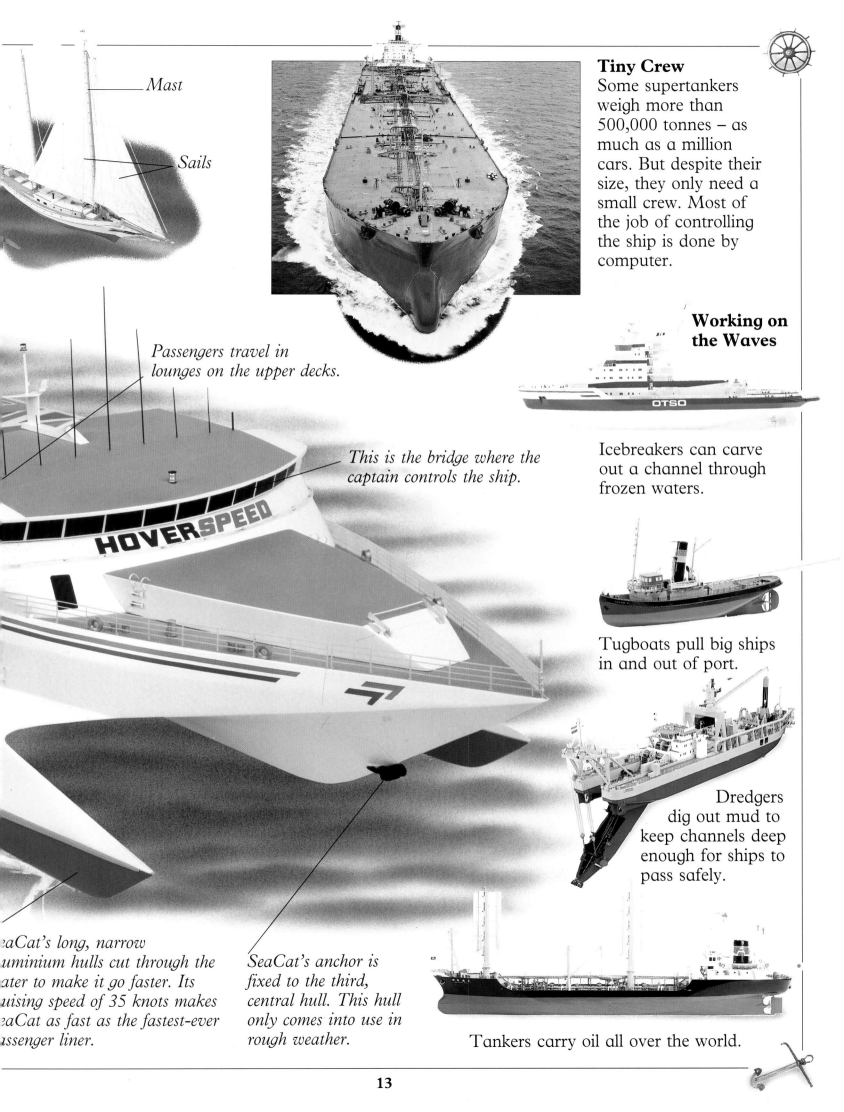

Mast

Sails

Tiny Crew
Some supertankers weigh more than 500,000 tonnes – as much as a million cars. But despite their size, they only need a small crew. Most of the job of controlling the ship is done by computer.

Passengers travel in lounges on the upper decks.

Working on the Waves

OTSO

This is the bridge where the captain controls the ship.

Icebreakers can carve out a channel through frozen waters.

HOVERSPEED

Tugboats pull big ships in and out of port.

Dredgers dig out mud to keep channels deep enough for ships to pass safely.

eaCat's long, narrow uminium hulls cut through the ater to make it go faster. Its uising speed of 35 knots makes eaCat as fast as the fastest-ever ssenger liner.

SeaCat's anchor is fixed to the third, central hull. This hull only comes into use in rough weather.

Tankers carry oil all over the world.

FLYING MACHINES

The simplest flying machine is a kite, which is swept up into the air by the wind. People were lifted off the ground by big kites in China 3,000 years ago. But kites only fly when the wind blows, and in any case are unlikely to take you where you want to go. To control your flight you need an engine to push or pull the plane along and so make its own wind.

Light, fabric wing

Lighter than Air

Hot-air balloons have a big bag of light material. When this bag gets big enough by being filled with hot air it becomes lighter than the surrounding air, so it rises. A gas burner controls how high the balloon goes. Heating the air inside makes the balloon expand and therefore rise. If the air inside gets cooler the balloon shrinks and sinks.

Battens to stiffen the wing

This is a microlight – the smallest aeroplane of all.

Wing is pushed up

Air flowing past the wing

How Wings Work

The wings of a plane are specially shaped so that the air flows faster over the top surface than over the bottom surface. This causes greater pressure on the bottom surface than on the top surface, so the wings are pushed up.

The propeller is turned by a small petrol engine.

Gas burner

Basket to carry passengers

The back wheels are on springs so that landing is not too bumpy.

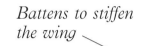

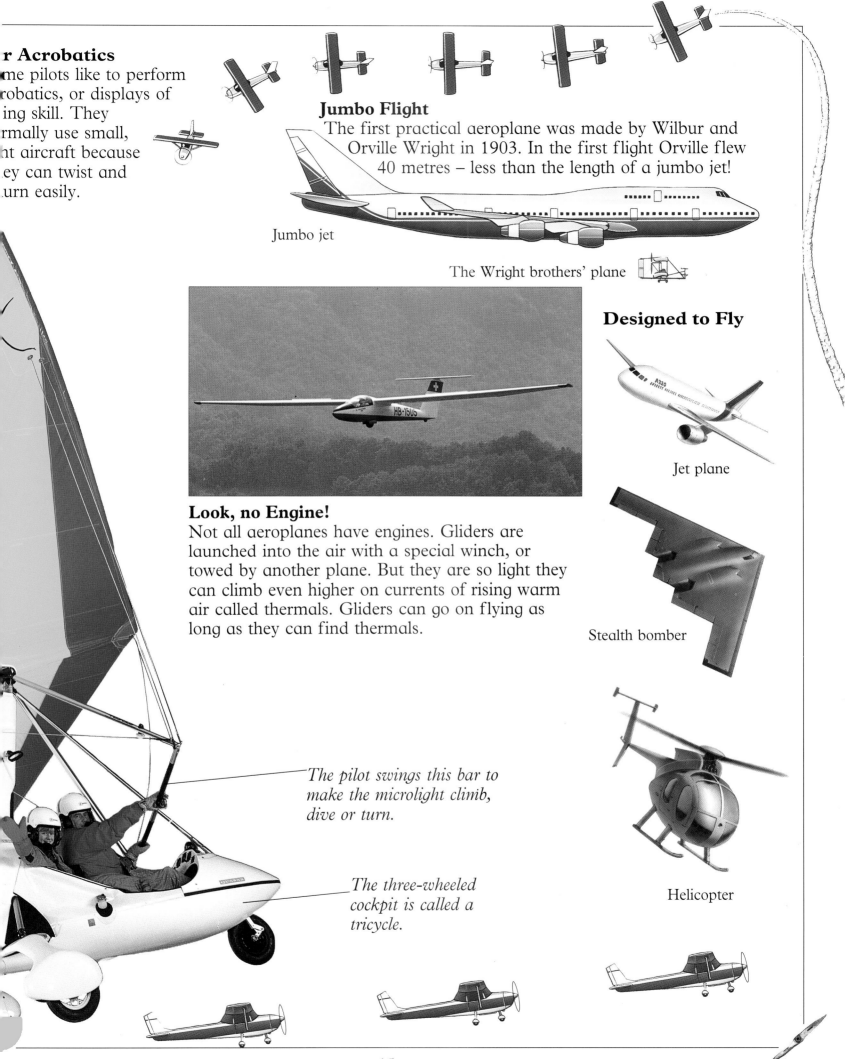

r Acrobatics

me pilots like to perform
robatics, or displays of
ing skill. They
rmally use small,
t aircraft because
ey can twist and
urn easily.

Jumbo Flight

The first practical aeroplane was made by Wilbur and
Orville Wright in 1903. In the first flight Orville flew
40 metres – less than the length of a jumbo jet!

Jumbo jet

The Wright brothers' plane

Designed to Fly

Jet plane

Stealth bomber

Look, no Engine!

Not all aeroplanes have engines. Gliders are
launched into the air with a special winch, or
towed by another plane. But they are so light they
can climb even higher on currents of rising warm
air called thermals. Gliders can go on flying as
long as they can find thermals.

Helicopter

*The pilot swings this bar to
make the microlight climb,
dive or turn.*

*The three-wheeled
cockpit is called a
tricycle.*

Machines for Power

Corn pours from this hopper into the narro space between grindstone surfa

The sails of a windmill are turned by the wind, just like a toy windmill when you blow on it. The wheel of a watermill is turned by a stream rushing past it. Windmills and watermills were the power stations of the past, providing the power needed for specially big or tiring tasks, like cutting stone or grinding corn. Now we use wind and water power to make electricity, and the electricity drives the machines that do jobs like these for us.

1. The water wheel has paddles that dip into the stream. The rushing water pushes on the paddles and turns the wheel.

Air Power
Windmills use the wind to drive their machinery. The top of this mill can be turned so that the sails are always facing the wind.

2. As the water wheel goes round, it turns a long rod or axle.

Water Power

Most watermills ground corn into flour, but they were also used for crushing olives, cutting marble, or even squeezing rags into paper.

6. These big flat stones are called grindstones. The upper one is turned by the main shaft. As it turns, the corn is crushed to flour between the two grindstones.

5. This is the main shaft. As the crown wheel turns, the main shaft turns with it.

4. This is the crown wheel. As the brake wheel turns, its teeth push the teeth of the crown wheel and turn it round.

3. Turning at the end of the axle is the brake wheel. All round its edge are teeth that slot into matching grooves on the crown wheel.

Gas Power

In gas-fired power stations, gas is burned to drive machines that make electricity.

Atom Power

In nuclear power stations, heat to make electricity comes from splitting atoms.

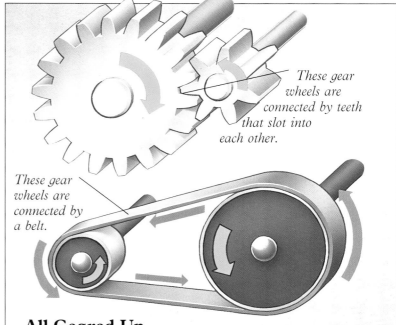

These gear wheels are connected by teeth that slot into each other.

These gear wheels are connected by a belt.

All Geared Up

Pairs of special wheels, called gears, can make machines go more slowly, more quickly, or more powerfully. If a small wheel turns a big wheel, the big wheel goes more slowly than the small one because it has farther to go round.

Strong Currents

Hydroelectric power is electricity made from rivers. The river water is collected behind a wall, or dam. Gates open to let the water rush into a tunnel where it turns special wheels that make the electricity. A lot of hydroelectric power is produced in countries with large rivers and high mountains.

DIGGING AND LIFTING

When you build a sandcastle on the beach you only need a tiny spade to dig out the sand. But to build factories, office blocks, bridges or tunnels, you need huge digging and lifting machines. Some are bigger than houses. Most have powerful arms and levers moved by hydraulics, and some are controlled by computers and guided by lasers.

Tunnel Giant
The tunnel linking Englan[d] and France is 50 kilomet[res] long and passes 40 metre[s] under the bed of the English Channel. Two machines, each 230 metr[es] long, were specially built [in] order to dig the tunnel.

Special rams push concrete linings into place to stop the rock falling in.

A conveyor belt carries the rock that is cut away out to the back of the machine.

Powerful hydraulic rams push the head forwards, and steer the machine.

To make the Channel tunnel, two of these boring machines, one at each end of the tunnel, slowly cut towards each other. They were guided by lasers so that they met up in the middle.

How Hydraulics Work

The arm of this mechanical digger is moved hydraulically. A pipe along the arm is filled with a special oil. When a piston pushes on the oil in one end of the pipe, the oil pushes another piston out at the far end with much greater force – enough to move the arm and its huge load.

Hydraulic piston

The bucket carves out the earth.

Wide tracks stop the digger from slipping, and keep it stable.

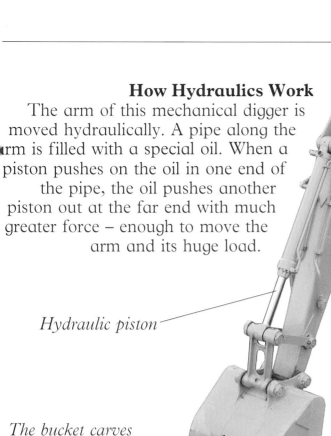

Towering Cranes

Tall cranes have a system of wheels, called pulleys, which means they can lift very heavy weights.

The cutting head has very hard teeth to cut through the rock. It turns round and round to grind the rock away.

Up and Away

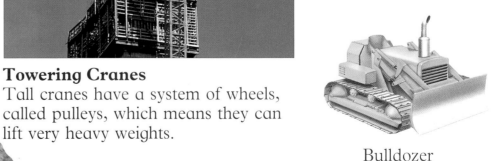

Fork-lift truck

Tipper truck

Bulldozer

Mechanical digger

TELLING THE TIME

Early mechanical clocks were not very accurate. Their gears were turned by a falling weight attached to an 'escape' wheel. The escape wheel made sure that the gears only moved or 'escaped' a little at a time. But the weight did not always fall at the same speed. So a pendulum, with its regular swing, was added to keep the escape wheel turning at a regular speed. In a modern clock, the steady beat that moves the gears comes from the vibrations of a piece of quartz crystal.

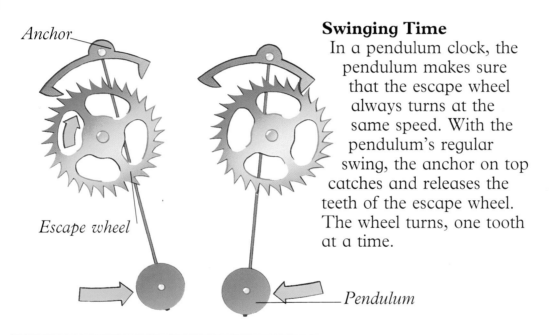

Anchor

Escape wheel

Pendulum

Swinging Time

In a pendulum clock, the pendulum makes sure that the escape wheel always turns at the same speed. With the pendulum's regular swing, the anchor on top catches and releases the teeth of the escape wheel. The wheel turns, one tooth at a time.

Pendulum Clock

This is a model of a very simple pendulum clock. It only has an hour hand so it is simpler inside than a real clock.

Clock face

Sun Time

As the sun moves through the sky, the shadows it casts move too. Long before clocks were invented, people used to tell the time by looking at the position of shadows. You can see this for yourself if you plant a stick in the ground and mark where its shadow falls at various times of day.

This heavy weight keeps the clock going. It is wound up to the top of the cable with a handle. The weight then falls slowly down again, pulling the escape wheel round as it goes.

This is the hour hand. If the clock had a minute hand, it would need its own gear wheel to turn it at a different speed from the hour hand.

The anchor on the swinging pendulum controls the turning escape wheel.

Crystal Time
When an electric current from a battery is sent through tiny crystals of a rock called quartz, the crystals vibrate very quickly. The vibrations are too small to see, but they are so regular that they are used to keep time in very accurate quartz watches.

Crystal of quartz

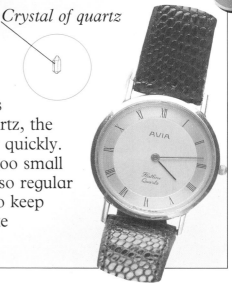

This is the escape wheel. It turns the main gear wheel.

The main gear wheel moves the hour hand round.

The pendulum swings to and fro with a regular beat.

The Big Time
One of the most accurate of all pendulum clocks is the clock in the tower of Big Ben in London.

Past Time
Before clocks with gears and pendulums were invented, people used all kinds of systems to keep track of time.

Water clock   Candle clock   Oil clock

Star clock

TAKING PICTURES

The autofocus measures how far away the subject of your photograph is, and adjusts the lens automatically.

Inside a camera is a roll of film that records all your photos one by one in a long strip. When you press the button to take a picture, a little door, or shutter, in the camera clicks open for a split second, letting light in to shine on the film. Special chemicals on the film record the pattern of light to make the picture.

The viewfinder is window through the camera to help you aim correctly.

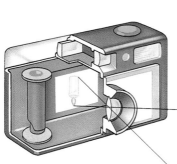

Light rays from the object in front of the camera pass through the lens. They reach the film to make a picture or 'image' on it.

The button you press to open the shutter and take a picture is called the shutter release.

This counter tells you how many pictures you have taken.

Instant Pictures
Polaroid cameras can give you pictures almost instantly. This is because all the chemicals needed to develop the photo are stored in a bulge at the end of each section of film.

You take your picture.

The picture is pushed out through rollers that squidge the chemicals from the bulge over the paper.

As the chemicals get to work, the picture starts to appear.

After a minute or two the picture is ready.

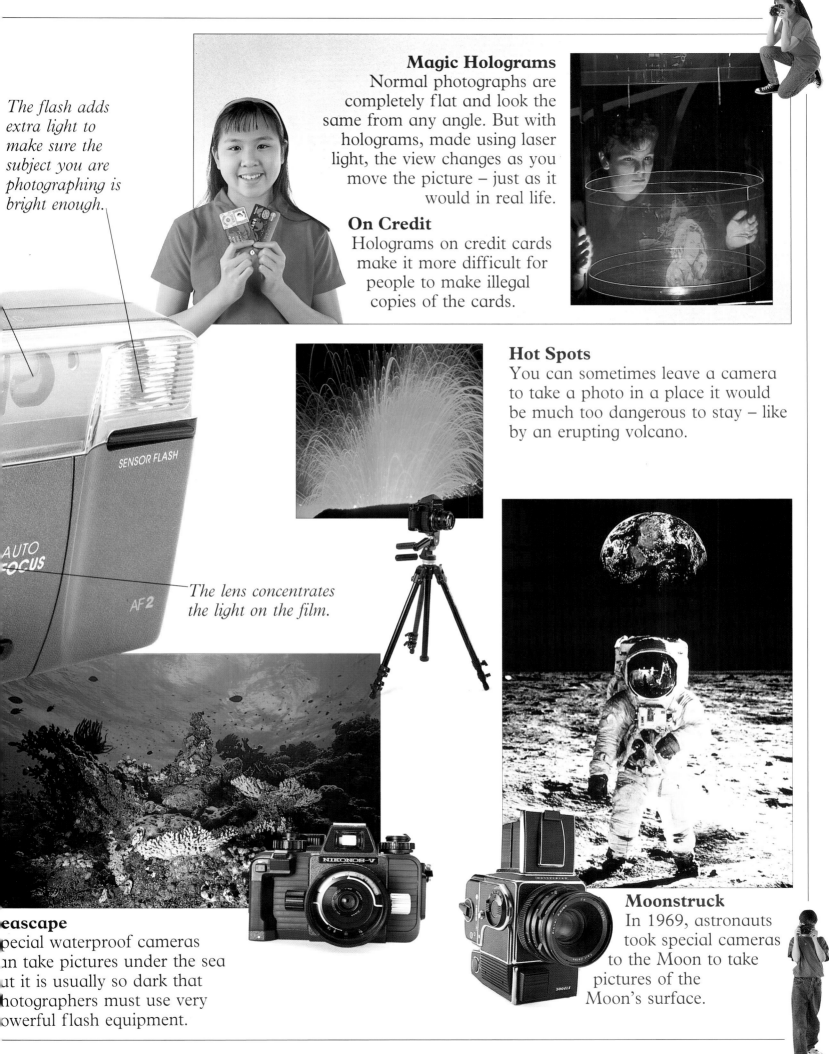

The flash adds extra light to make sure the subject you are photographing is bright enough.

Magic Holograms

Normal photographs are completely flat and look the same from any angle. But with holograms, made using laser light, the view changes as you move the picture – just as it would in real life.

On Credit

Holograms on credit cards make it more difficult for people to make illegal copies of the cards.

SENSOR FLASH

AUTO FOCUS

AF 2

The lens concentrates the light on the film.

Hot Spots

You can sometimes leave a camera to take a photo in a place it would be much too dangerous to stay – like by an erupting volcano.

NIKONOS-V

eascape

pecial waterproof cameras n take pictures under the sea ut it is usually so dark that hotographers must use very owerful flash equipment.

Moonstruck

In 1969, astronauts took special cameras to the Moon to take pictures of the Moon's surface.

MAKING MOVIES

When you watch a film, people and things on the screen seem to move as naturally as if they were real. Yet what you are seeing is actually a series of thousands of still photographs, or 'frames'. But the frames change so quickly it looks just as if the people and things are moving.

If the projector – the machine that shines the film onto the screen – were slowed down, you would see each of these still photographs going past, one by one.

Reel Life

Even a reel of film lasting just a few minutes has many thousands of pictures. Each picture is very small, but the projector magnifies it to fill the cinema screen.

As the film passes through the projector, a light shines through the frames, one by one, projecting them onto the screen.

Shutter open

Moving the Film

In a movie camera there is a special shutter. This turns to let light reach the film, one frame at a time, as the film runs quickly through the gate.

Gate

Shutter closed

Each time the shutter closes, a swinging claw slots into a hole along the side of the film and pulls the next frame into position. Projectors have a similar claw to move the film through.

Swinging claw

Film is stored in circular cans.

Moving Dinosaurs

Weird creatures in movies like *The Dinosaurs* can be a lot of fun to watch. They look realistic but in fact are latex models. Special, computer-controlled, electric motors inside them make them move just like real-life animals.

When the Dinosaur smiles, a computer instructs dozens of little electric motors to move different parts of his face.

© The Walt Disney Company

Editing a Film

When a movie is shot, the sound is recorded on special, separate tapes. The editor uses an editing table to make sure that the pictures and sounds match when film and sound are put together.

The film starts on this reel.

Screen to view pictures

Spool of film with pictures

Loudspeaker

Spool with recorded speech

Spool with recorded sound effects

Disaster!

Film makers can use special effects to create the weather they want or to make dangerous things happen safely. Here gas jets – just like those in a coal-effect gas fire – are used to make it look as if a building is being burned down.

A lens magnifies the picture so that it fills the screen.

Every second, 24 frames pass through the projector.

As the movie is shown, the film is gradually wound onto the take-up reel.

The Big Screen

You can watch a film on the big screen at a cinema, or on a small home-movie screen in your living room. The pictures you see are actually the reflected images of the pictures on the film. The light in the projector throws the images onto the screen.

The screen is usually made of special white material to make the picture bright and clear.

SPREADING THE NEWS

Television can bring news of events happening far away, like a war or a football match. Pictures and sounds are recorded on tape, then turned into radio waves and bounced to you right round the world off satellites in space. Radio, newspapers and magazines bring you world news too, and your own fax machine or videophone can keep you up to date with your personal news.

A 'sun gun' lights the scene, like the flash on a still camera.

The on-camera microphone record background noise.

Signals from the sound man's audio mixer are received here and recorded on the tape with the picture.

Recording tape

News in Print
Teams of newspaper and magazine journalists and designers set out their stories on computer screens. The words are printed on a special film. Another computer scans the pictures and makes picture film. The printer uses both sets of film to print the text and pictures onto paper.

The camera operator carries a lightweight camera. Inside are thousands of special dots or cells that record each part of the scene as an electric current on tape.

The sound man can chec through these headphones that he has 'mixed' the sound proper

Making film using a computerised scanner

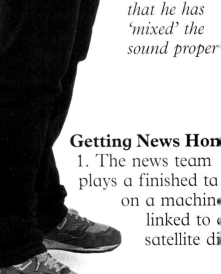

Getting News Hom
1. The news team plays a finished ta on a machin linked to satellite di

26

See You on the Phone

When you call someone on a videophone you can see them as well as hear them, thanks to a special TV camera. The picture is sent as an electric signal along a wire, just like the voice on an ordinary phone.

The boom, or shotgun microphone, gets close to the sound that the sound man is recording.

News Machines

There are many different ways of sending and receiving information.

Police radio   Citizens' Band radio

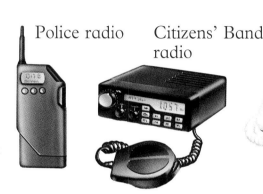

Fax machine

The audio mixer is used to make sure that the sound being recorded can be heard clearly against any background noise.

4. At the news centre the news team mixes the story in with other news and sends it to the transmitter.

5. You see the pictures on television when the aerial on your house picks up the radio waves from the transmitter.

3. The signals bounce off a satellite down to the news centre.

2. The dish beams the signals up into space.

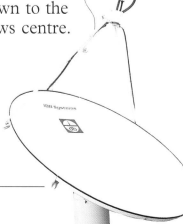

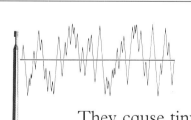

Making Waves

Radio waves are invisible ripples sent out by a transmitter. They cause tiny electrical vibrations in the aerial on your TV or radio. These vibrations change an electric current in your set into sounds and pictures.

WAR MACHINES

An aircraft carrier

Hand grenade

Modern armies have all sorts of weapons, from rifles and grenades for fighting a single enemy, to bombs and missiles for attacking large targets. Soldiers can g into battle riding in a tank – a huge gun on wheels protected by heavy armour plating. But nothing can protect against nuclear bombs, the most powerful weapons of all.

Going Bang!

Gunpowder was first used in China about 1,000 years ago for making fireworks.

In 1605, Guy Fawkes tried to blow up the English Parliament with gunpowder.

In 1867, Alfred Nobel invented a very powerful explosive called dynamite.

The main gun can fire powerful shells that will travel 3,000 metres.

This is the turret. It turns round so the gun can be aimed in any direction.

The tank can carry a huge amount of fuel – around 1,900 litres. But it is only enough to drive about 440 kilometres at 40 kilometres an hour.

The commander sits at the top.

The driver sits inside at the front and uses mirrors to see what is happening outside.

The gunner aims the main gun using a thermal imaging sight. This picks up the heat given out by enemy targets.

The loader loads the main gun with explosive shells. He also operates the radio

nway at Sea

craft carriers are huge ships
h flat decks which war
nes use for taking off and
ding. The carriers sail close
enemy coasts so the planes
n launch attacks.

*Ine of the crew uses a
achine gun to defend
he tank against
nemy aircraft.*

Muskets were used by soldiers in the 17th
century. They needed reloading after each shot.

*Heavy steel armour
up to 13 cm thick
protects the crew
from enemy fire.*

Hand-guns like this
Colt 45 were carried about
150 years ago by cowboys in
the American west. They
could fire six bullets without
being reloaded.

Automatic machine guns
were invented in 1884 by
Sir Hiram Maxim. They
could fire dozens of
bullets one after the other.

*The wheels run
inside tough metal
bands called caterpillar
tracks. To steer, the
driver makes one track run
faster than the other.*

*Destruction caused by a
nuclear bomb in Hiroshima,
Japan, 1945*

Nuclear Weapons
A single nuclear
bomb can destroy a
whole city, and the
radiation it leaves
behind can kill
people and animals
years later. There
are now enough
nuclear weapons to
destroy the world.

A Nuclear Explosion

. As the bomb explodes
 makes a
 ant
 reball.

2. The
explosion
shakes
the city
below.

3. The
blast
and fire
destroy
buildings.

4. Rubble and
dust mushroom
up high into
the sky.

SPYING AND SNOOPING

Spies make it their business to find out other people's secrets and they have an array of sneaky devices to help them. Tiny radio transmitters or 'bugs' can be hidden in a room to listen in on private conversations. Video recorders can be concealed in books and briefcases to take pictures without anyone knowing. There are special goggles and cameras to spot things in the dark, and if you think someone is cheating on you, there are clever gadgets to help you find out.

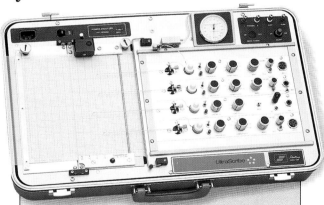

Are you Lying?

Lying often makes people sweat more or breathe more quickly, or makes their heart beat faster. Liars can be caught out by using a lie detector to spot these changes.

I Spy

Two people meet to chat in an ordinary room. But is it an ordinary room? Is it an ordinary conversation? There is more here than meets the eye.

Green fingers? Hidden in the pot plant is a tiny tape recorder to record the conversation with your visitor.

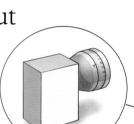

Can you read between the lines? No bigger than a matchbox, this video camera can be slipped inside a book for secret filming.

Is she tricking you? A voice stress analyser hidden in the desk may alert you to tell-tale tremors in her voice.

It looks like an ordinary briefcase. In fact it is a secret video recorder. The lens is a tiny hole in the side and the controls to start recording are in the handle.

...e you receiving me?
...ur boss can give you
...tructions without anyone
...owing, using an ear spy –
...iny radio receiver that
...invisibly inside
...ur ear.

Fact or Fantasy?
In the fantasy world of spy films anything can happen. James Bond's car could squirt oil or fire drawing pins from the rear lights. A bullet-proof panel helped protect him, extendable bumpers could ram other cars, and radar in the wing mirrors kept track of enemy cars.

The lighter patches show the warm engines of the cars that arrived most recently at this car park.

If you are discovered and your enemy has a gun, the bullet-proof vest hidden under your clothes may save your life.

Seeing Red
A 'thermal imaging' camera spots warm things, even in the dark. It shows in colour the invisible infrared rays given out when something gets hot. The lighter the colour, the warmer the object being viewed.

Hidden inside the door knob is a tiny 'bug' that picks up all sounds in the room and radios them back to base.

A view through night-vision goggles

If you are in trouble, you can secretly summon help with this pen. It contains a tiny radio transmitter that sends a bleep back to base in emergencies.

Cat's Eyes
You can see in the dark with these special night-vision goggles which pick up even the tiniest traces of light.

COMPUTER MAGIC

Computers are the world's cleverest machines. Inside a computer are thousands of very tiny electronic switches, a bit like light switches. By switching them on and off in different combinations, computers can perform all kinds of tasks. They are used every day in car factories, hospitals, supermarkets and offices. Some guide aircraft, ships, submarines and spacecraft. Others, like virtual reality machines, can be for fun, to take you on exciting imaginary voyages.

The headset has a mini TV screen in front of each eye and a speaker over each ear.

When you move your head, this cable sends signals to the computer.

In a virtual reality machine you can imagine you are at the controls of a jump jet, a spacecraft or even a mechanical dinosaur.

Keeping your Head Up
A jet fighter pilot must not take his eyes off the view ahead, even for a second. All the information he needs to control the plane and fire at targets is fed to a computer and projected onto the pilot's face mask. This is called a 'head-up' display.

Feeling the Way
Doctors can use virtual reality gloves to look inside you before they decide to operate. As they run their hands over you, sensors in the gloves send signals to a computer. The computer makes a 3-D picture of your insides on a little TV screen in the doctors' headsets.

is cable carries signals
m the computer for the
tures and sounds in
    headset.

When you turn
your head,
different views
come up on the
TV screens in
the headset.

Pocket Brain
Fifty years ago, the
first computers filled
a large room. Now
an equally clever
computer can be
the same size as
a pocket calculator.

Bytes and Megabytes
Computers can help
with homework or
get an astronaut to
the Moon.

Calculator

Laptop computer

Shrinking Switches
The switches in
computers have got
steadily smaller
and more complicated.

*The first computers
had big glass valves.*

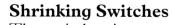

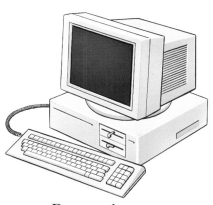

Personal computer

*Computers now have
tiny microprocessors.*

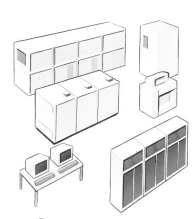

Super computer

*Electric motors rock the virtual reality machine
backwards and forwards and from side to side
to make your 'journey' more realistic.*

VIRTUALITY

ROBOTS

Robots are machines that 'think' with a computer brain which tells them what to do. Once they have been programmed, they can work entirely by themselves. Some people believe that one day we will be able to make robots that can do everything a human can – and they may even look like humans. At the moment, though, most robots are nothing more than mechanical arms or cranes.

Mechanical Men

Automata are clever machines that move rather like humans or animals. This one was made for a fair in Victorian times.

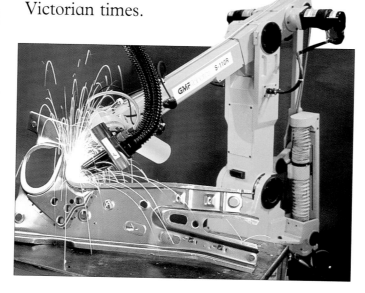

Factory Hand

A factory robot is often just a moving arm. But a robotic arm can hold things, screw them into place, weld them and check that they work. It can replace lots of human workers.

An electronic voice allows the robot to answer and ask simple questions. It can also obey some clearly spoken commands.

Robots at Work and Play

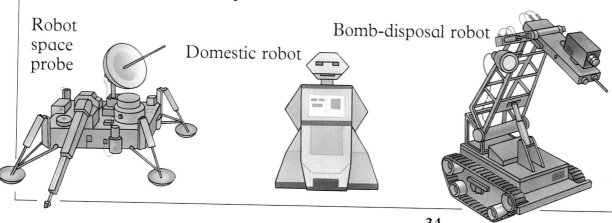

Robot space probe

Domestic robot

Bomb-disposal robot

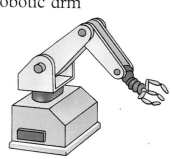

Robotic arm

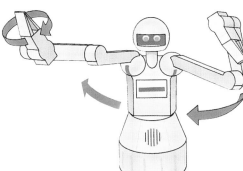

The robot can pick up your newspaper by squeezing its claws together. Its 'muscles' are powered by electric motors.

Each of the claws has special pressure sensors so that they do not crush things they pick up.

Electronic eyes allow the robot to spot obstacles in its path and steer round them.

The robot's brain is a powerful computer. It tells the robot what to do by sending electronic signals to the motors that move the robot's different parts.

Robogymnast
The robot can turn its hands and move its arms. But unlike a human, it can turn its arms right round.

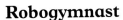

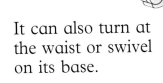

It can also turn at the waist or swivel on its base.

Home Help
A robot like this is really just a clever toy. But one day there may be robots that can do the shopping, cleaning and other household chores for you.

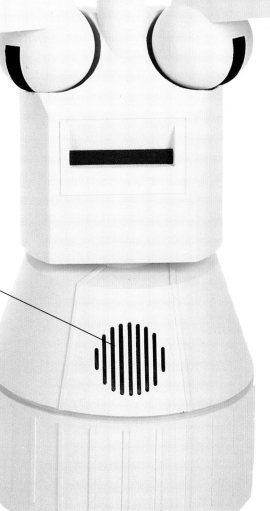

Like Humans?
Manny is a lifelike robot with computers that can make it 'sweat' and 'breathe'. Scientists use Manny to test special clothing like spacesuits and firefighting clothes. If Manny can 'breathe' and doesn't 'sweat' too much, then the clothes will be safe for a human to wear.

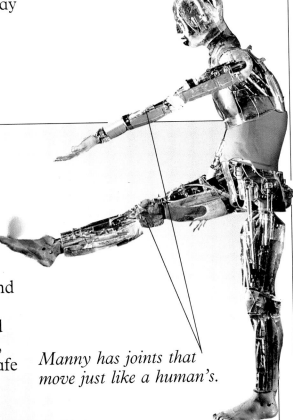

Manny has joints that move just like a human's.

MACHINES FOR HEALTH

This is an MRI scan that has had colours added.

If you have to visit your doctor or go to hospital, you will see that doctors use lots of machines to help them find out what is wrong with you. There are simple machines to check your blood pressure or listen to your chest. There are also the really complicated ones like the huge electronic scanning machines, which can take pictures of the inside of the body – showing anything from a baby growing in its mother's womb to what goes on in your brain.

First Sounds

A pregnant woman may be given ultrasound scans to see if her baby is growing well. These use sounds that are too high for us to hear. When the sounds are beamed into the mother's womb, a computer analyses the way they are reflected to create a picture of the baby inside.

The patient can be moved backwards and forwards on the sliding table for different parts of the body to be viewed.

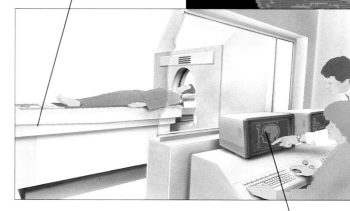

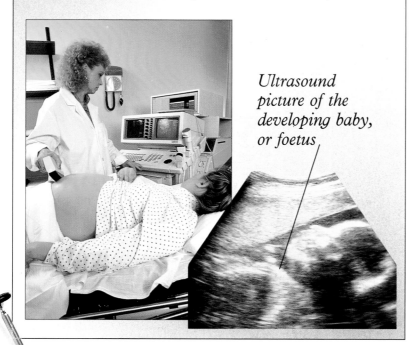

Ultrasound picture of the developing baby, or foetus

The image is displayed on a computer screen.

Magnetic Resonance Imaging

MRI is a safe way of getting a picture of what is going on inside someone. The patient lies in a ring of magnets so powerful that the body's atoms are pulled into line, like tiny rows of magnets. If they are knocked briefly out of line by a strong radio signal, they send out little radio waves. These are used by a computer to build up the picture.

Look Inside?

Doctors use many instruments to see inside you and check if there is anything the matter.

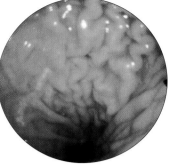
Stomach viewed with an endoscope

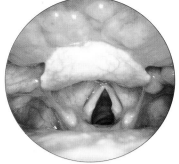
Vocal cords viewed with a laryngoscope

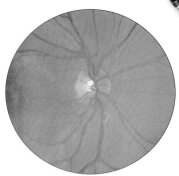
Inside the eye viewed with an ophthalmoscope

Listening In

A stethoscope is a listening tube. With it, a doctor can hear the sounds made by your heart and lungs. It will help the doctor decide what is wrong with you.

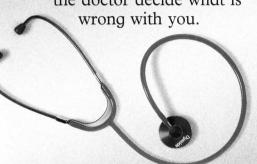

X-Ray Vision

X-rays are a bit like light rays but they pass through skin as easily as light shines through glass. They do not pass through bones though, and an X-ray picture shows the shadows of bones. Your dentist might take an X-ray of your teeth to see if they are growing correctly.

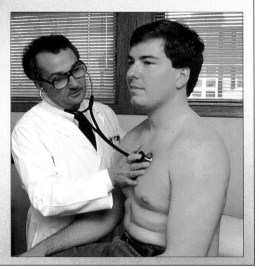

This X-ray of a boy's second teeth shows he has tooth decay.

Brain Slice

MRI gives doctors very clear pictures. It can be used to spot heart problems and abnormal growths in the brain so that they can be operated on.

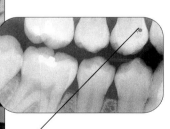

X-Ray Arm

By looking at this X-ray picture of a broken arm, the doctor can see exactly where the damage is and can decide how to treat it.

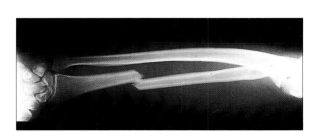

HOME HELPS

Before gas and electricity, people used open fires to cook and to keep warm, they read by candlelight, and got down on their hands and knees to clean the carpet. Now, in many parts of the world, homes and gardens are full of machines that make life easier, safe, and more comfortable. With the time we save doing household chores, we can groom ourselves from top to toe with a choice of electrical gadgets.

Outdoor lights wi[th] sensors can turn themselves on whe[n] someone comes ne[ar]. Burglars beware!

You can plug a special vacuum cleaner into a socket in each room. The dust is sucked away through hidden pipes to a waste bin.

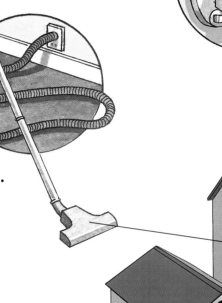

Power Gardening

There are lots of machines to help in the garden. Strimmers, or nylon-line trimmers, cut grass in awkward corners, hedge trimmers take the effort out of keeping a hedge tidy, and chainsaws are for sawing large branches. Robot lawnmowers can cut the grass automatically.

As you drive up to your garage you can press a button in your car to open the electronically controlled garage door.

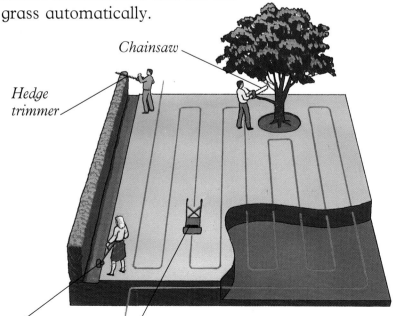

Chainsaw

Hedge trimmer

Strimmer, or nylon-line trimmer

A robot lawnmower has sensors that follow a cable buried under the lawn. The mower cuts the grass automatically as it follows the cable.

Your cat can wear a special tag on its collar. The tag opens the catflap for it – but keeps strange cats firmly locked out.

Smoke detectors set off an alarm to warn if there is smoke in your home. They can help you to stop a fire spreading.

In Control

Thermostats in greenhouses keep plants at the right temperature because plants, like people, do not like to be too hot or too cold. A thermostat turns the heat off if it gets too warm, and on if it gets too cold.

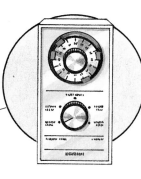

This timer controls the heating. It automatically switches the heating on and off at whatever times you want during the day.

Time for Yourself

There are all sorts of machines you can use to look after yourself. You can curl your hair with a hot-air brush and clean your teeth with an electric toothbrush. Some people shave with an electric razor, tone their muscles with electronic slimming pads, then round off their tiring day using an electric foot massager.

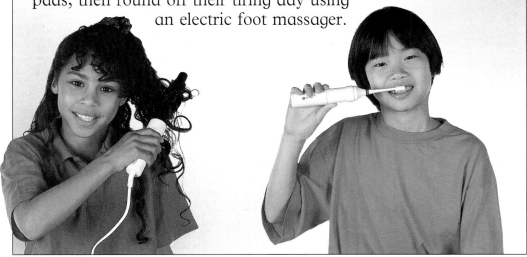

Kitchen and Laundry

We use many machines to help store or cook food, and to clean clothes.

Refrigerator

Washing machine

Electric stove

Electric coffee filter

SPORTS MACHINES

In the past, sport was rather simple. Often, a bat and ball were all you needed. Today there are many fantastic machines for sport. In bowling alleys machines reset the pins after each throw, on tennis courts machines check electronically where the balls bounce, and on mountain sides there are machines for making snow for skiers. Even fencing, which used to be for killing an enemy, is now a sport with electric equipment to help judge who is the winner.

Finger holes in the ball make it easier to grip.

Display screens tell you how many pins you have knocked down and give the score.

Making Snow
People love playing in snow – but sometimes there just isn't enough of it. Many ski resorts have machines to make artificial snow for skiers. These snow machines use a special cold gas that turns water into powdery ice. The ice is pumped out through a nozzle onto the slopes.

On the Line
Electronic sensors buried beneath the lines on a tennis court can tell if a ball bounces inside the court. The ball is coated with iron powder and the sensors detect it as it passes over. If the ball is out, a bleep goes off.

Most bowling centres ha lots of lanes so that man people can play at once.

After each ball, the pins that have been bowled over are cleared away. Automatic grips hold the others in place.

At the end of your turn, all the pins are cleared away then set down in exactly the right places, ready for the next bowler.

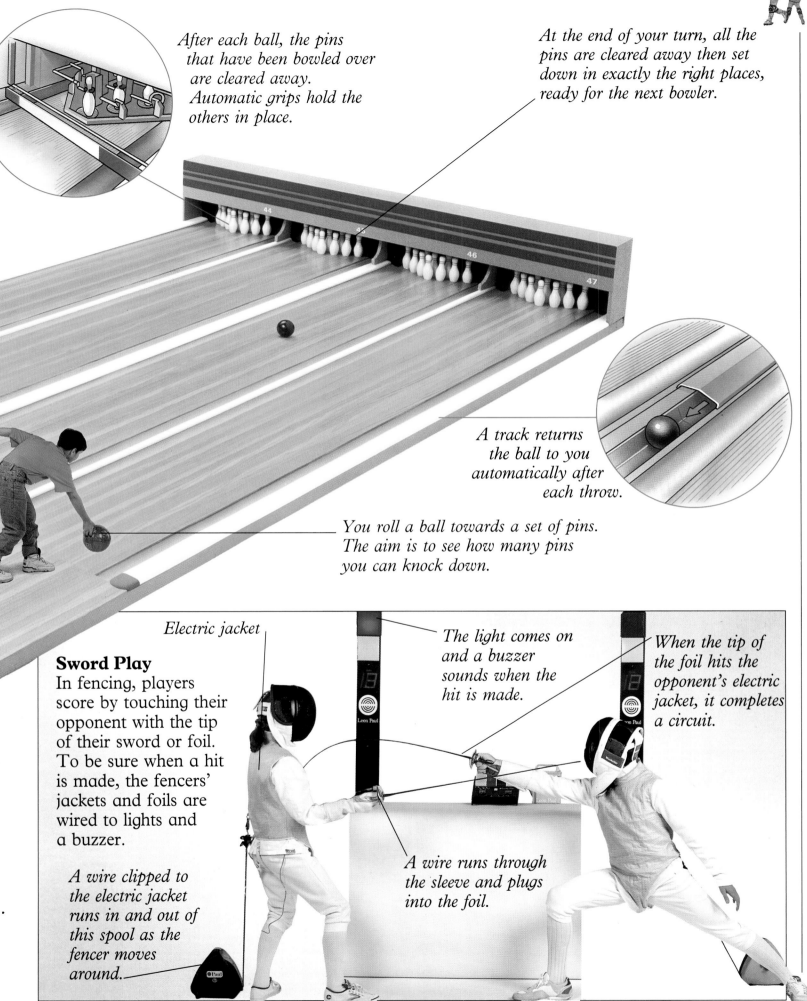

A track returns the ball to you automatically after each throw.

You roll a ball towards a set of pins. The aim is to see how many pins you can knock down.

Sword Play
In fencing, players score by touching their opponent with the tip of their sword or foil. To be sure when a hit is made, the fencers' jackets and foils are wired to lights and a buzzer.

A wire clipped to the electric jacket runs in and out of this spool as the fencer moves around.

Electric jacket

The light comes on and a buzzer sounds when the hit is made.

When the tip of the foil hits the opponent's electric jacket, it completes a circuit.

A wire runs through the sleeve and plugs into the foil.

ELECTRONIC GAMES

The custom chip keeps track of the score and controls the screen display

At the heart of every electronic game, there is a tiny block or chip, called a processor. Inside the chip are thousands of little electronic circuits. Whenever a light flashes or a spaceship moves across the game screen, it is the circuits that are making it happen. Some games, like electronic chess, have their circuits set at the factory so the circuits cannot change. But in hand-held video games, you put in a disk, and the disk controls the circuits. Each disk makes the circuits work in a different way and gives you a new game to play.

Remote control

You press the start button to switch the machine on.

The cross-shaped direction button gives you control over the movement of figures on the screen.

The aerial sends out beams of radio waves to the car.

Remote Control

The controls of a remote-controlled model car, plane or boat send out beams of radio waves.

A tiny radio on the model picks up the waves and switches on an electric current. The current operates the model's little electric motors, or servos. The servos steer the model or make it go faster or slower.

You press this select button to choose your game and skill level.

The loudspeaker makes the sound effects.

Radio receiver in model

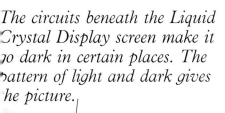

The circuits beneath the Liquid Crystal Display screen make it go dark in certain places. The pattern of light and dark gives the picture.

The processor chip sends a stream of electronic signals to the circuits beneath the screen.

DOT MATRIX WITH STEREO SOUND

Information from the game disk is fed into the processor chip.

The circuits of the processor chip control the game.

These buttons control firing, rotating and jumping.

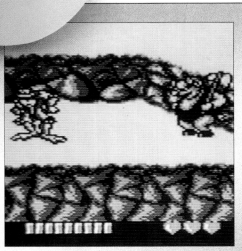

On Display

Video games have an LCD, or Liquid Crystal Display, screen made up of thousands of small squares. Beneath each square is a tiny liquid crystal and a mirror that reflects light. When an electric current is sent through the crystal, the crystal twists and blocks the reflection, making that square dark. The picture is built up from light and dark squares.

Electronic Toys

Electronics are used in many of the toys you play with. Even a game like chess, that has been around for hundreds of years, can now be played electronically.

Electronic chess

Infrared screen control gun

Table-top soccer game

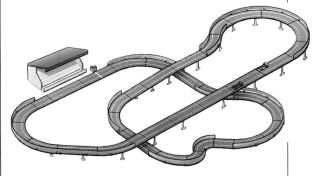

Racing car game

MAKING MUSIC

Over 40,000 years ago, people discovered they could carve animal horns to make musical instruments such as flutes. Since then, thousands of different musical instruments have been created, from simple whistles to grand pianos, each with its own special sound. Now, as well as making music, we can also listen to recorded music any time we want, thanks to electronic machines like personal stereos and CD players.

The longer strings at this end give deeper notes.

Pressing keys at this end gives very deep notes.

These pedals al... the sound slight... making it sof... or loude...

Very Grand Piano
The piano is one of the biggest instruments and one of the most popular. You can use both hands together to play many notes at the same time, so its sound can be very dramatic.

Sounds in the Air
When you play an instrument, the surrounding air is stretched and squeezed again and again. You hear the sound because these squeezings and stretchings – known as sound waves – travel through the air and vibrate your eardrums.

Hammer Action
When you press on a piano key, a lever lifts a jack. The jack raises a soft-headed hammer that hits a taut metal string, making it vibrate. The string vibrates the air to make the sound we hear.

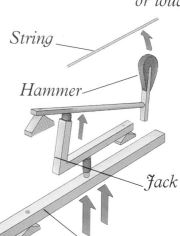

String

Hammer

Jack

Lever

Key

A Museum of Music

Waxed cylinder
music player

Phonograph

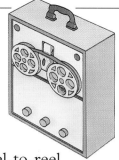

Reel-to-reel
tape recorder

Radio recorder

Portable CD player

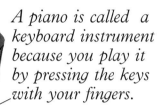

The shorter strings at this end give higher notes.

A piano is called a keyboard instrument because you play it by pressing the keys with your fingers.

Pressing keys at this end gives high notes.

The black and white wooden strips are called keys. When you press them, they make the strings inside the piano vibrate.

Electronic Keyboards

An electronic keyboard is played like a piano, but it works very differently. A piano's sound comes from vibrating strings. An electronic keyboard's sound is made with tiny electronic vibrations. It can mimic all kinds of instruments.

Sounds Special

A trumpet is a brass instrument played by blowing with pursed lips.

A recorder is a woodwind instrument played by blowing through a shaped mouthpiece.

A violin is a string instrument played by vibrating the strings with a bow.

FAIRGROUNDS

Fairgrounds are full of colourful, fantastic machines to thrill you and make you laugh. The first big fairground machines were the merry-go-rounds or carousels of about 120 years ago.

These beautiful, steam-driven roundabouts, with gaily painted horses, turned to the sound of an automatic steam-driven organ. The rollercoasters, waltzers and big wheels of today are driven by powerful diesel engines, or electric motors. Rides get more spectacular and more exciting every day!

A seat or bucket

A powerful motor in the middle drives the moving floor round.

Coloured lights flash on and off as the waltzer spins round.

Pinned to your Seat

When you whirl a ball round on a string, you feel it pulling away. Let go of the string, and the ball will go flying off in a straight line. This effect, called centrifugal force, keeps you in your seat in a rollercoaster, even when you are upside down. Just like the ball, your body tries to carry on in a straight line as the car loops round, so you are pressed into your seat.

Centrifugal force keeps pushing the bucket – and you – outwards.

The bucket can spin, but is held firmly in place on the floor.

...ding High

...is still possible to
...nd old-fashioned
...erry-go-rounds
...th their painted
...rses, even in a
...odern fairground.

Rollercoasters

Rollercoasters hurtle you round in loops and up and down terrifying slopes. Wheels above and below the track hold the cars in place, and centrifugal force keeps you in your seat – even when you are travelling upside down at 130 km/h.

Big wheel

The outer floor of the waltzer stays still.

The central platform has hinged sections that allow it to bend up and down as it goes around.

Teacup ride

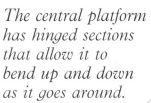

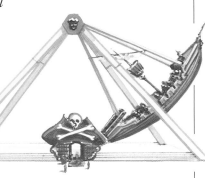

Pirate swingboat

Bright Lights

...t needs a lot of electric
power to keep fairs
...rightly lit. Fairgrounds
make their own
electricity, using noisy,
big, diesel-driven
generators on lorries.

Dodgem car

GLOSSARY

Aerial A rod or a loop of wire connected to a TV or radio that picks up signals from the air.

Atom The tiniest bit of a substance. It can only be seen under a very powerful microscope.

Circuit The loop of wire around which an electric current flows.

Combustion A scientific word that means burning.

Compressed air Air squashed into a small container. It can be let out in a jet strong enough to drive tools like drills.

Computer An electronic machine for processing information. It can do anything, from simple sums to guiding a spacecraft.

Crankshaft In an engine, a rod with a series of right-angled bends called cranks. As the pistons of the engine go up and down they turn the crankshaft round and round.

Diesel engine A type of engine often used in lorries and buses. Diesel fuel is exploded simply by squashing it in the cylinder.

Electric current A steady flow of electricity through a wire.

Electronic Controlled by electric circuits that are switched on and off with tiny switches like transistors. Silicon chips are minute electronic circuits.

Hull The shell of a ship that sits in the water.

Jack A tool used for lifting heavy things.

Laser An intense beam of light that can be used as a cutting tool to perform delicate eye surgery or to blast holes through steel.

Lens A specially shaped disc of glass that focuses, or brings together, light rays to form a picture.

Magnet A piece of steel with magnetic power – the invisible force that pulls other magnets towards it or pushes them away.

Meter A tool for measuring things, for example, how much gas you have used.

Microphone A device that turns sounds, such as voices, into an electrical signal.

Microprocessor A tiny package of complicated electronic circuits. Microprocessors are the most important part of computers and other electronic devices.

Propeller The whirling blades that drive ships and some aeroplanes along.

Radar A scanner which sends out a beam of radio signals to find out where ships and aeroplanes are.

Radiation Energy spreading outwards. Light is a kind of radiation. So are the rays given out by nuclear bombs and nuclear power stations.

Satellite A man-made machine that circles the Earth high up in space. It can bounce TV signals and phone calls around the world or send back pictures of the Earth for weather forecasts.

Scan A means of building up a digital picture of something by running sound over it.

Sensor A machine that detects change, for example a change in heat or pressure.

Space probe A kind of spacecraft sent far off into space under computer and radio control.

Supertanker A giant oil tanker. Supertankers are the biggest ships in the world.

Traction engine An old steam engine used for pulling heavy weights, like ploughs.

Virtual reality The illusion of reality created by a computer headset.

Acknowledgments

Photography: Steve Gorton, David Rudkin Studios, James Stevenson.

Illustrations: The Colour Company, Roy Flooks, Peter Griffiths, Ray Hutchins, Norman Lacey, Linden Artists, Patrick Mulray, Sebastian Quigly, Peter Serjeant.

Models: Cheltenham Cutaway Exhibits Ltd, Donks Models, Peter Griffiths.

Thanks to: Norrie Carr Child Model Agency; Dakar Cars; Sue Duffey; Mr A.F. Gueterbock and the Eurotunnel Exhibition Centre; Imperial War Museum; JCB (UK) Ltd; Simon Markson and Markson Pianos; The Old Sarum Flying Club; Leon Paul Equipment Company Ltd; Reuters Televison Ltd; Scallywags Child Model Agency; Sea Containers Services Ltd; Mr K.J. Selwood; T.L.M; Wessex Microlytes; W. Industries, Leicester, for the loan of a 'Virtuality' machine.

Picture credits

Aviation Picture Library: Austin J. Brown 14c, back jacket; **British Aerospace:** 32bl; **Brookes and Vernons/JCB:** 2-3c, 4cra, 18tl, 18bl, 19tc; **Bruce Coleman:** Eric Crichton 16clb, Geoff Dore 17tl, Graham Jennings 47bc, Nancy Sefton 23clb; **Lupe Cunha:** 37cb; **The Walt Disney Co.:** 25tc; **Mary Evans:** 28clb; **Game Boy/Battle Toads:** 43bl; **Ronald Grant Archive:** Warner Bros - *Robin Hood, Prince Of Thieves* 6cl; **Sonia Halliday:** 7tl; **Robert Harding:** 23tl; **Robert Hunt Library:** 29br; **Hutchison Library:** Julia Davey 46tr; **Image Bank:** 36tl, Ronald Johnson 17tc, Rob Atkins 23crb, Nino Mascardi endpapers, Benn Mitchell 36tl, Jurgen Vogt 19c; **Impact:** Mike McQueen 28cla; **Kobal:** 25tc; **Jaeger-LeCoultre:** 21crb; **Magnum:** Erich Hartmann 31br; **MARS/US Navy:** 28tr; **The Mews Dental Surgery:** 37cbr; **Museum of Automata, York ©:** 34cl; **National Motor Museum, Beaulieu:** 31tc; **Panos:** J. Hartley 6br; **Popperfoto:** 33tc; **Professional Sport:** 40bc; **Science Photo Library:** Alex Bartel 28bl, Professor C. Ferlaud/CNRI 37tc, Malcolm Fielding/Johnson Matthey PLC 26bl, Lowell Georgia 1c, Adam Hart-Davies 31cr, Mehau Kulyk 5bcl, 36-7c, Rory McClenaghan 37tr, Peter Menzel 32bc, Larry Mulvehill 36bl, Hank Morgan 37bl, 37cr, Philippe Plailly 23cra, St. Bartholomew's Hospital 36bc, Dr. Klaus Schiller 37tl, James Stevenson 37bc, Takeshi Takahara 9tc, Sheila Terry 34c, US Dept. of Energy 35br; **Harry Smith:** 39tc; **Snow Machines Inc.:** 40clb; **Telegraph Colour Library:** 10br; **Zefa:** 3c, 13tc, 15c, 17tr, 17bcl, 21cr, 47tl.

Every effort has been made to trace the copyright holders and we apologize in advance for any unintentional omissions. We would be pleased to insert the appropriate acknowledgments in any subsequent edition of this publication.

t – **top**	l – **left**	a – **above**	cb – **centre below**	
b – **bottom**	r – **right**	c – **centre**	clb – **centre left below**	crb – **centre right below**

NDEX

rial 27, 42
rcraft carrier 28, 29
chor 20, 21
mour plating 28, 29
dio mixer 26, 27
tomata 34
le 8, 16, 17

ttery 21
ach buggy 8-9
g Ben 21
g wheel 47
om 27
ring machine 6
w and arrow 6
wling alley 40-41
gging device 30, 31
lldozer 19

mera 22, 23, 24, 26,
7, 30
rs 8, 9, 11
tamaran 12, 13
terpillar tracks 29
D player 44, 45
ntrifugal force 46, 47
annel tunnel 18
ema 24, 25
rcuit 35, 41, 42, 43
ty of Truro train 9
cks 20-21
ckpit 15
mpressed air 12
mputer 13, 18, 25,
6, 32-33, 36
mputer switches 33
ne 19
ankshaft 11
edit cards 23
linder 11

fferential 8
dgem car 47
edger 13
namite 28

iting table 25
ctricity 10, 16, 17, 21,
5, 26, 27, 33, 42, 43
ctronics 32, 38, 42, 43

engines 8, 9, 10-11,
  12, 14, 46
English Channel 12, 18
escape wheel 20, 21

F

fairground 10, 46-47
Fawkes, Guy 28
fax machine 26, 27
fencing 40, 41
film 22, 24, 25
film projector 24-25
fireworks 28
flash 23
fork-lift truck 19
fuel 10, 11, 14, 47
fulcrum 7

G

game disc 42, 43
gears 8, 17, 20, 21
generator 47
glider 15
greenhouse 39
gunpowder 28
guns 28, 29

H

hairdrier 10
hand-gun 29
headphones 26
helicopter 15
hologram 23
hot-air balloon 14
hull 12, 13
hydraulics 18, 19
hydroelectric power 17

I

icebreaker 13

J

jet engines 10, 11
jet plane 11, 15

K

keys 44, 45
keyboard 45

L

laser 18, 23
lens 22, 23, 25
lever 7
lie detector 30
liquid crystal
  display (LCD) 43
loudspeaker 25, 42

M

machine gun 29
magnet 10, 36
magnetic resonance
  imaging (MRI) 36, 37
mechanical digger 19
merry-go-round 46, 47
microlight 14-15
microphone 27
Model T Ford 9
motors 10-11, 25, 33,
  42, 46
musket 29

N

night-vision goggles 31
Nobel, Alfred 28
nuclear bomb 28, 29

P

pendulum 20, 21
piano 44-45
pilot 15, 32
pirate swingboat 47
piston 11, 19
planes 10-11, 14-15
plough 6
power stations 16, 17
processor chip 42, 43
projector 24, 25
propeller 14
pulley 19

Q

quartz 20, 21

R

radar 31
radiation 29
radio 27, 28, 30,
  31, 36, 42, 45
recorder 45
reel 24, 25
robots 34-35

S

sails 12, 16
satellite 26, 27
scissors 6, 7
screwdriver 6, 7
SeaCat 12-13
sensor 34, 38
servo 42
ships 12-13, 28, 29
shutter 22, 23, 24
skiing 40
smoke detector 39
snow machines 40

sound waves 44
spanner 7
spark plug 11
spies 30
Stealth bomber 15
stereo player 44
stethoscope 37
strings 44
submarine 12
supertanker 12, 13

T

tank 28-29
tap 7
tape recorder 30
teacup ride 47
television 26, 27
tennis 40
TGV 9
thermal imaging 28, 31
thermals 15
thermostat 39
timer 39
tipper truck 19
traction engine 10
trains 8-9
transmitter 27
Trevithick, Richard 8
trumpet 45
tugboat 13

U

ultrasound 36

V

vibration 20, 21, 27, 45
video camera 30
video game 43
videophone 26, 27
violin 45
virtual reality machines
  32-33
voice stress analyser 30
Volkswagen Beetle 9

W

waltzer 46, 47
watermill 16
wheel 6, 7, 8, 9, 14, 16,
  17, 29, 47
wind 9, 12, 14, 16
wind tunnel 9
windmill 16
Wright brothers 15

X

X-ray 37